BRINGING BIBLE CHARACTERS TO LIFE

Building Learning Centers about Old Testament Bible Characters

for Children, Ages 6-12

Written by: Sheri Gittins
Cover Illustration by: Mike Denman
Inside Art by: Kathlee Bogart

TO THE TEACHER:
About Learning Centers

Below are some guidelines that address questions you may have about LEARNING CENTERS:

WHAT IS A LEARNING CENTER?

A learning center is a space in a classroom that is set aside for individual or small group instruction. This area may be a desk, small table, place on the floor, or the corner of a room. It does not need to be elaborate or big. The center can be stationary or mobile, depending on the varied use of your room.

The center needs to contain an activity complete with instructions and supplies. Every time a new center is created, a few minutes should be utilized to explain the directions for using the center. Such directions help the children to understand what they are supposed to do, and create an interest in the center.

WHEN AND HOW ARE LEARNING CENTERS USED?

Learning centers can be used at various intervals during your class time. Children arriving early can work at a center, thus helping to alleviate boredom or discipline problems. Another time a learning center can be used is when children are engaged in individual activities. While some individual children work, others can rotate in and out of the center. Children who complete work early or who may have extra time can use the center to better utilize their time spent in Sunday school.

Groups can also use learning centers. Group work is especially useful when you have large classes. You can divide the class into smaller groups, have one group as a reading group, for example, and another group can work at the learning center.

Learning centers can be left in place for several class sessions so that children can benefit from reviewing what they have learned from previous Sunday school classes. Make sure the center has plenty of supplies and materials throughout the Sunday school sessions. When more than one center is in place, you may want to keep a timer in the room and have children select another activity when the timer goes off. This allows more children to participate in a variety of activities.

WHAT IF THE CHILDREN CANNOT READ THE STORIES THEMSELVES?

Each Bible story has been re-written for an audience of children between the ages of six and twelve. However, if some of the younger children have difficulty reading the material, you can read the story to them. Another idea is to have an older child read the story, or the stories can be recorded. Then the tape player can be placed at the learning center with the volume turned on low. The children can listen to the stories and still do the activities at the learning centers.

HOW DO I STORE MY LEARNING CENTERS?

Most learning center materials can be stored in ziplock bags or large brown envelopes. Simply label the containers according to the titles of the centers.

TABLE OF CONTENTS

"NOAH'S ARK"

Scripture: Genesis 5-9:17

Once there was a man named Noah. Noah was 600 years old! He lived during a time when many people were very wicked. They would do mean things to each other. Noah was a good man, though. He talked to God, and God shared back to Noah. Because Noah was a good man, he also taught his sons to be good. This pleased God very much.

One day God told Noah about a plan He had to destroy the earth and all of the evil in the world. He also promised Noah that his family would not be hurt. If Noah listened to God, God would help Noah and his family to stay safe.

So God told Noah to build a huge ark out of gopher wood. Once the ark was built, Noah was told to take his family and put them on the ark and live on it. Noah was also supposed to take two of every animal and put them on the ark. God then told Noah that a huge rainstorm would come and cover the entire world. Everybody and everything on the ark would be safe.

Then it began raining. It rained for forty days and forty nights. The world was completely covered with water for 150 days!

Then one day Noah let out a dove. Several days later the dove returned, and it had a green olive leaf in its mouth. Noah knew that the floods had gone down and that they could very soon leave the ark.

Finally God spoke to Noah. He told Noah that he could go outside, and to take his family and the animals. Noah did so, and everyone was safe. Noah prayed to God and thanked God for taking care of him and his family.

God promised Noah that He would never send a flood to destroy the world again. Instead, He promised that He would have changing seasons. He put a rainbow in the sky to tell people of His promise.

LEARNING CENTER:

Use a file folder as a game board. Use stickers, labels cut in half, or draw circles to create a path across the inside of an open file folder. Use paper clips as markers. They clip right to the file when not in use. You can make your game last longer if once you are finished creating it, you laminate it or cover it with clear Contac® paper. You can decorate the outside of the folder to use with a particular subject, or leave it plain to use over and over. A board pattern is on page 6.

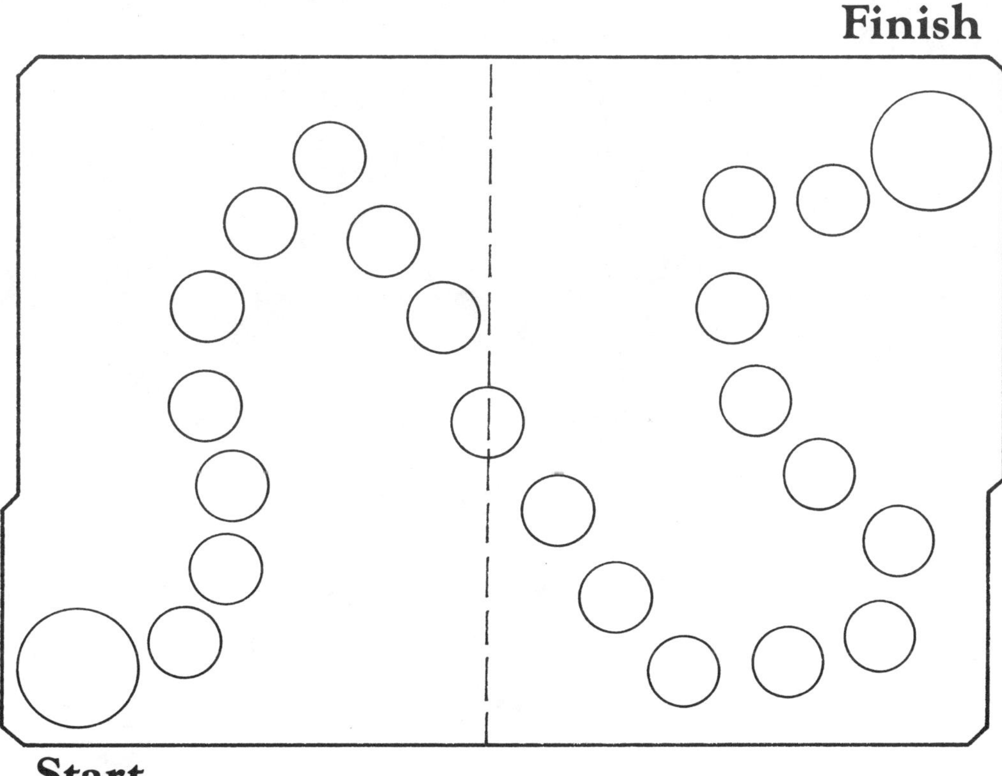

You can copy the question card page or simply cut the page from the book. You can cut out the answer key or record the answers on the back of each card. It is important to include the directions with your game cards and answer key. You can store all of these items in a ziplock bag.

Directions:

Read the Bible story. You may use your Bible while answering the questions. If you answer correctly, you may move 2 spaces.

Answer Key:

1. man was wicked
2. he found favor with God
3. earth
4. gopher
5. flood
6. 2
7. 40 days and 40 nights
8. 600 years
9. 150 days
10. Noah and his family

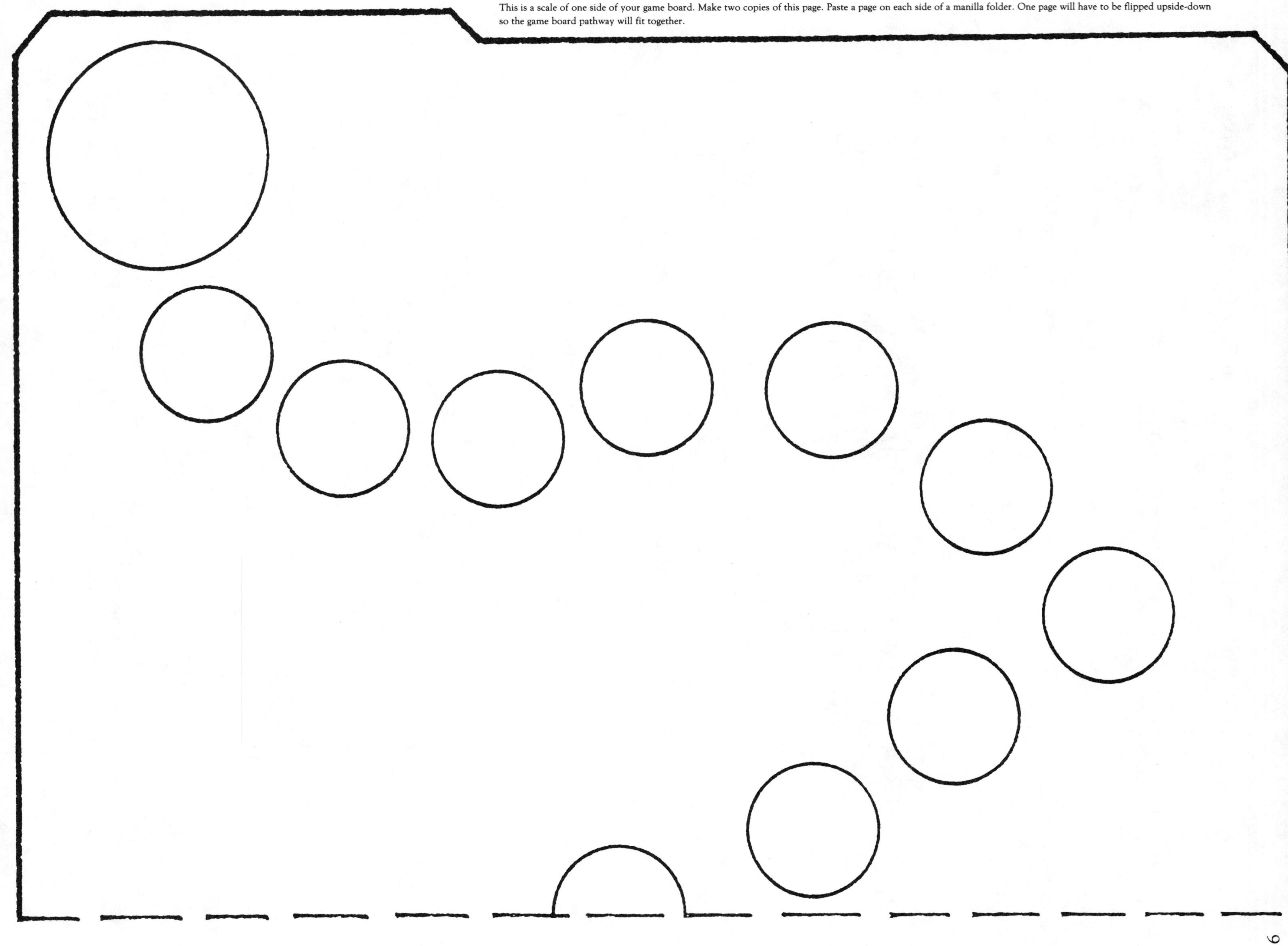

This is a scale of one side of your game board. Make two copies of this page. Paste a page on each side of a manilla folder. One page will have to be flipped upside-down so the game board pathway will fit together.

1. Why was the Lord sorry He had made man?	6. How many of each animal were on the ark?
2. Why did God let Noah live?	7. How long did it rain?
3. God decided to destroy the ____________.	8. How old was Noah when it began to rain?
4. God told Noah to build an ark out of ________ wood.	9. How long did the earth stay covered in water?
5. How did God destroy the earth?	10. What people lived through the flood and were blessed by God?
Free Card Move 1 Space	

GAME CARDS FOR NOAH AND THE ARK

"DANIEL PRAYS TO GOD"

Scripture: Daniel 6

Daniel was a very respected leader in his kingdom. He obeyed God and was a good man. Darius, the king, decided to put Daniel in charge of the whole kingdom. This made the other leaders jealous.

So the leaders decided to find something that Daniel was doing wrong so he would not get promoted. They couldn't find any fault with Daniel because he trusted and obeyed God. The jealous leaders talked the king into passing a law that said people could only make requests to King Darius. The leaders knew that Daniel prayed to God, and so he would get in trouble. The law said if anyone disobeyed the king's order by praying to another god, then they would be thrown into the lions' den.

The next day, the jealous leaders waited outside Daniel's house until they heard him praying to God. Then they told King Darius that Daniel disobeyed his law. Darius was sad because he liked Daniel, but he still had to throw him into the lions' den.

The next morning when the king returned to the den, he found Daniel alive. God had saved Daniel from the hungry lions! The king threw the jealous leaders into the lions' den, and they were eaten. The king then made a new law saying that Daniel's God was the the living God.

LEARNING CENTER:

Copy the lions on a copy machine. Color them and write "true" or "false" on the back of each lion according to the answer key provided. Copy the story on the previous page. You may want to glue it to cardboard to make it more durable.

Directions: Read the lions. Decide if the statement is true or false. The answers are on the back of each lion.

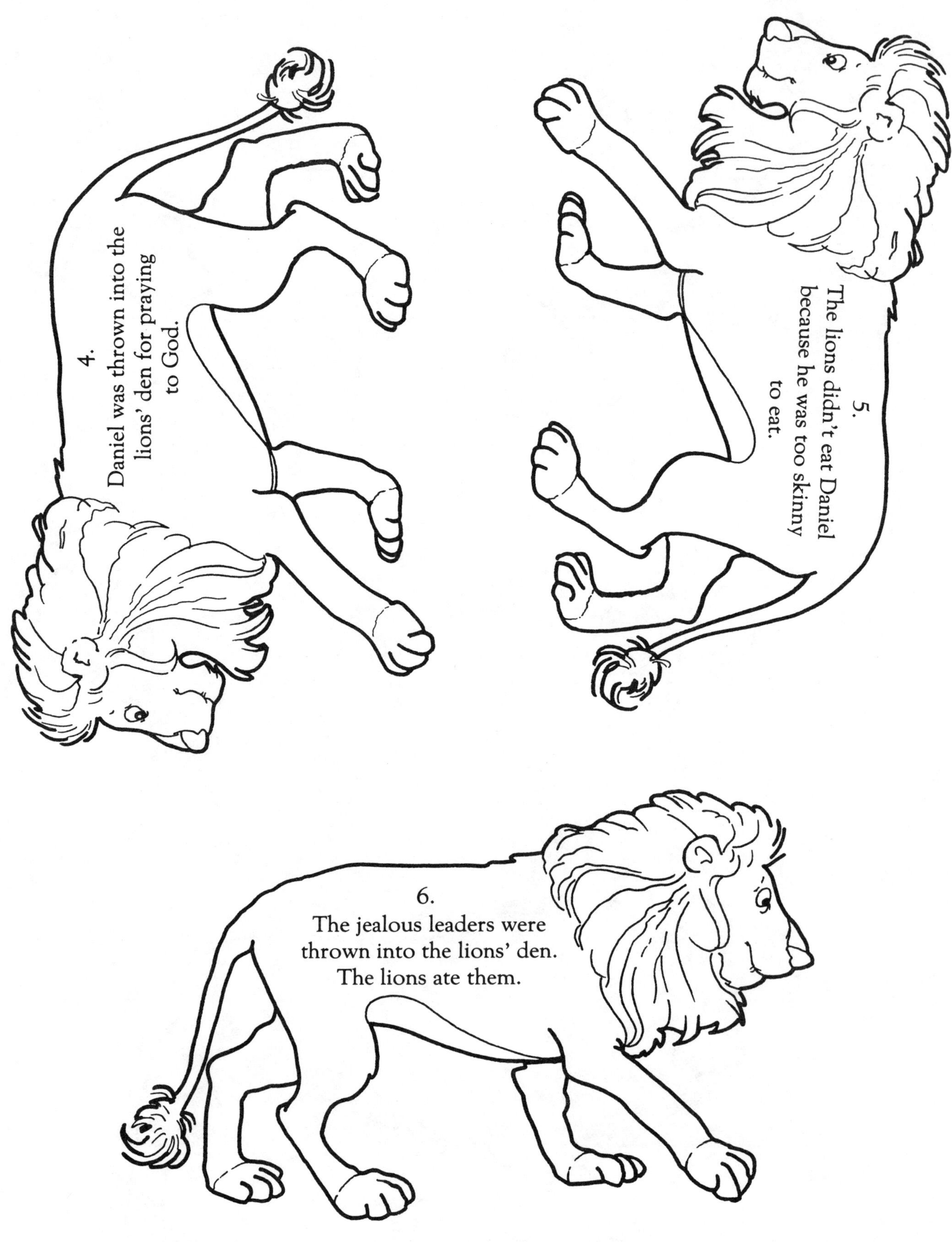
4.
Daniel was thrown into the
lions' den for praying
to God.
5.
The lions didn't eat Daniel
because he was too skinny
to eat.
6.
The jealous leaders were
thrown into the lions' den.
The lions ate them.

Answer Key:

1. False	5. False
2. False	6. True
3. True	7. True
4. True	8. False

You can store this center in a ziplock storage bag or a big brown envelope. Just label the outside of the container.

"DAVID TAKES A STAND"
Scripture: 1 Samuel 17:1-54

Goliath was a mean giant. He was a Philistine. The Philistines and the Israelites were fighting against each other. Goliath said that if anyone from Israel could fight him and kill him, then the Philistines would become servants of the Israelites. If Goliath won, then Israel would become servants for the Philistines. The Israelites were very scared because nobody wanted to fight Goliath.

David was a shepherd boy who loved and served God. One day, he was bringing food to his brothers who were fighting in the battle, when he heard Goliath challenging the Israelites. David volunteered to fight Goliath because he knew God would help him. When King Saul heard about David, he didn't want David to fight. He told David he was too small and young to kill the giant. But David convinced Saul that he could do it with God's help.

So David went to fight Goliath. Goliath had a spear and heavy armor, but David just wore his regular clothes and took five stones and a slingshot. David put one stone into his sling and shot it toward Goliath. The rock sank into the giant's forehead, and Goliath fell to the ground! David grabbed Goliath's sword and killed him. And then David thanked God for helping him to destroy the mean giant.

LEARNING CENTER:

You can copy, color, and cut out David, Goliath, and the stones. You will want to copy the story "David Takes a Stand." You can use the Answer Key to record the answers on the back of the stones.

Directions: Place the stones that describe Goliath on the giant. Place stones that describe David on the boy. The answers are on the back. Now read, "David Takes A Stand."

Answer Key:

1. Goliath	5. David
2. David	6. Goliath
3. Goliath	7. David
4. Goliath	8. David

Goliath

David

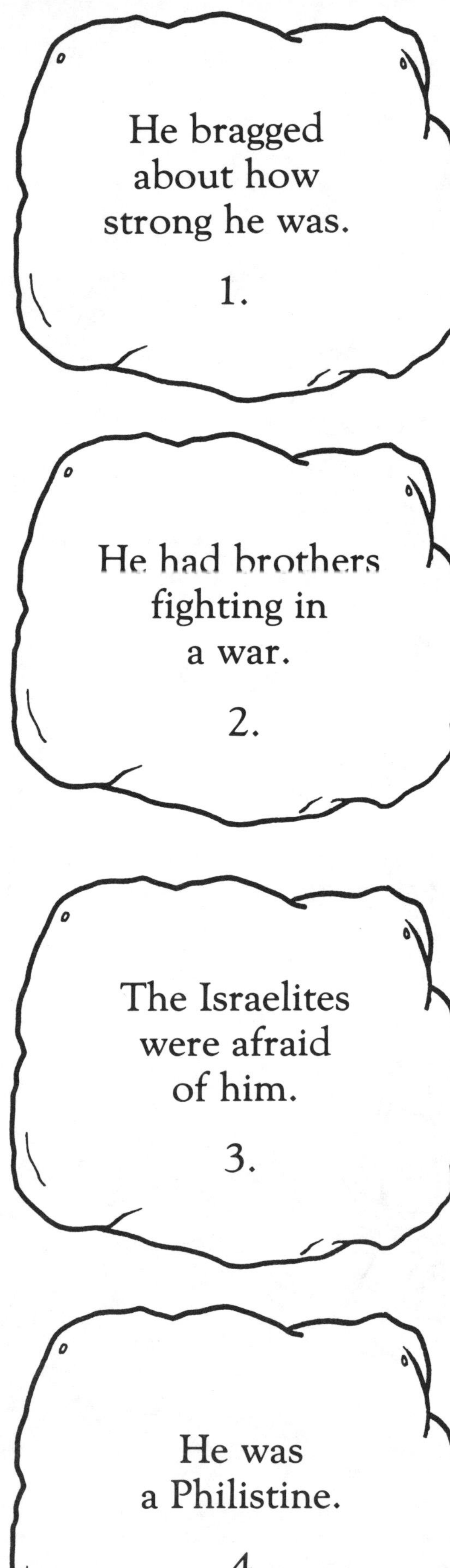
He bragged
about how
strong he was.
1.
He had brothers
fighting in
a war.
2.
The Israelites
were afraid
of him.
3.
He was
a Philistine.
4.

He
trusted
God.
5.
He used
dangerous
weapons.
6.
He won
the battle.
7.
He volunteered
to fight because
he knew God
wanted to
help him.
8.

"IN THE GARDEN"

Scripture: Genesis 2:8-3:24

When God created the world, He made a man and a woman, Adam and Eve. God put Adam and Eve in charge of everything on the earth. He gave them a beautiful garden to live in. It was perfect! God told Adam and Eve they could eat anything that grew in the garden except fruit from a certain tree.

One day Adam fell asleep. While he was sleeping, the devil who pretended to be a snake started talking to Eve. He told her if she ate the fruit God told her not to eat, she would be wise. So Eve ate the fruit. When Adam awakened, she gave some of the fruit to Adam, and he ate it, too.

That evening Adam and Eve heard God walking in the garden. They hid from God because they knew they had disobeyed Him. God called to them and asked them why they were hiding. Adam and Eve told God about what they had done.

God made Adam and Eve leave the perfect place. He told them that because they had disobeyed His words, they would have to work and plant crops to survive. And so Adam and Eve had to live with the outcome of their bad decision to disobey God.

LEARNING CENTER:

Copy the story from page 17. Copy, color and cut out the apples. You may want to glue the apples to poster board (and cut them out again) to make them more sturdy. Record the answers on the back by matching the numbers on the apples (2 matching apples would both have a 1 on the back).

Directions: Every choice you make has a bad or good consequence. Here are apples with choices and consequences. The apples with choices have numbers on them. The apples without numbers on the front are consequences. Match the choices with the correct consequence. The answers are on the back of the apples. Read the story, "In the Garden."

Answer Key:

1. You feel good about helping one of God's creatures.
2. Your parents find out about your poor choice.
3. You feel sad that someone else is getting in trouble.
4. People like to be friends with kids who are nice.

On the way
to a friend's house
you see a kitten
caught in a thorn bush.
You are in a hurry,
but you decide to stop
and help the kitten.

1.

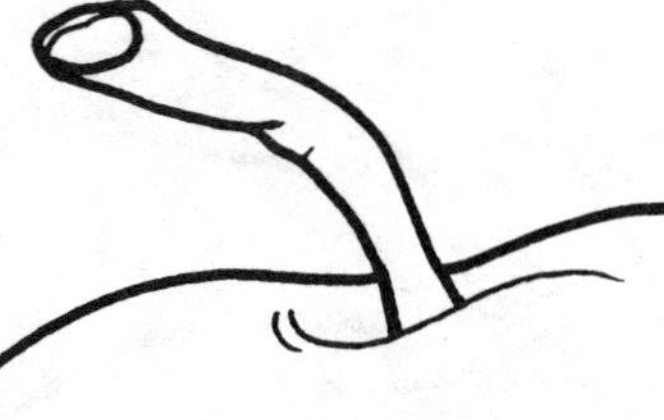

You feel good
about helping one of
God's creatures. God is
smiling because you made
a good choice.

Your good
friend tells you he
didn't have time to study for a
test. He asks you if he can copy
from your paper. You don't want
him to be mad so you say yes.
During the test other kids
keep watching you.

2.

Your parents
find out about your poor choice.
They ground you and make you
tell your teacher what you did.
You feel embarrassed
and ashamed.

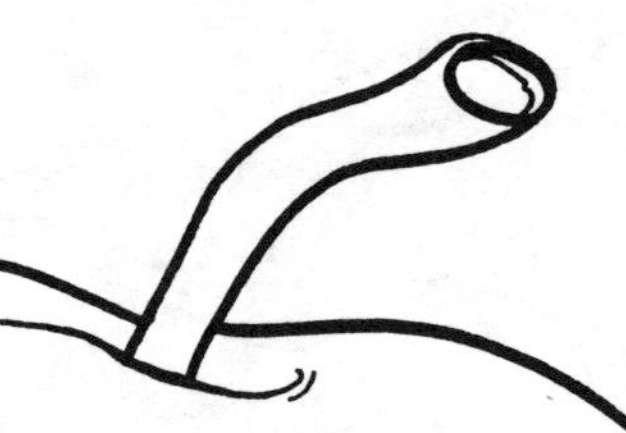

You accidentally break your mom's favorite dish. She blames your younger brother. You know if you tell the truth you'll get in trouble. So you don't say anything.

3.

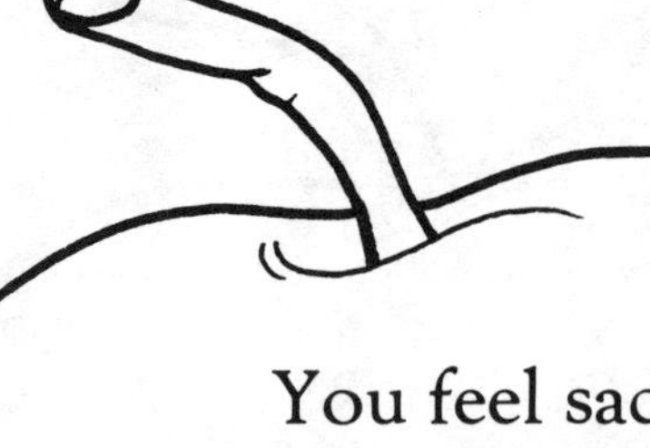

You feel sad that someone else is getting in trouble for what you did. That person knows you did it and will have a hard time believing or trusting you.

You see a new kid in school. She doesn't know anybody, and she is standing all by herself at recess. You are having fun with your friends, but you decide to go over and invite her to play.

4.

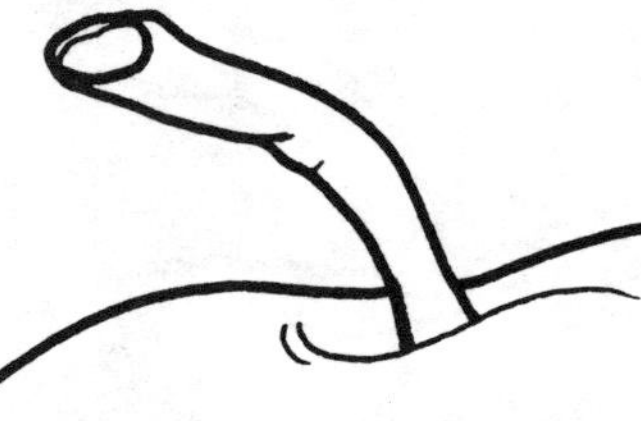

People like to be friends with kids who are nice. You feel good about helping people and making friends.

"JONAH RUNS FROM GOD"

Scripture: Jonah 1, 2

God spoke to Jonah and told him to go to a city called Nineveh. God wanted Jonah to go there to tell the people to turn from their wicked ways. Jonah did not want to go, so he tried to run away from God. He went to the seashore and hid in a ship.

God knew where Jonah was, and He caused a great storm in the sea. The ship was tossing, and waves were coming into the boat. The sailors were scared, and prayed to their gods. But Jonah was asleep. The sailors awakened Jonah and told him to pray. Jonah knew why there was such a terrible storm. He told the crew that he was hiding from God.

Jonah told the sailors to throw him into the sea so that the storm would quit. So the sailors threw Jonah into the sea, and God made the waters calm. Then God told a giant fish to swallow Jonah. Jonah lived in the belly of the fish for three days and three nights. Finally Jonah prayed to God and said he would do what God wanted him to do.

The fish spit Jonah out onto the land. Jonah went to Nineveh and gave them God's message. God blessed Jonah for obeying Him. And Jonah learned that he could never run away from God.

LEARNING CENTER:

This center is for 2-4 learners. Copy the story from page 21. Copy, color, and cut out the whales. Copy and cut out the game cards. You will want to record the answers from the Answer Key on the back of the cards.

Directions: Each player has a whale. Place the cards question-side up in the middle of the table. Take turns picking a card. If you answer a question correctly, place the card on your whale. The player with the most cards wins. Read the story carefully. The answers are on the back of the cards.

Answer Key:

1. Nineveh
2. A ship
3. He didn't want to go to Nineveh.
4. A terrible storm
5. Sleeping
6. Jonah was hiding from God.
7. They threw him into the sea.
8. A giant fish swallowed him.
9. Jonah prayed to God.
10. The fish spit him out.
11. He went to Nineveh.
12. No
13. Yes

1. Where did God want Jonah to go?	8. What happened to Jonah once he was in the sea?
2. Where did Jonah run away to?	9. What happened after 3 days and 3 nights?
3. Why did Jonah try to run away from God?	10. How did Jonah finally get to dry land?
4. What happened that scared the sailors?	11. What did Jonah finally do?
5. What was Jonah doing while the sailors were praying?	12. Can you ever run away from God?
6. Why was there such an awful storm?	13. Did Jonah make the right decision in the end?
7. What did the sailors do to Jonah when he told them the truth?	

Whales for Jonah Game

Whales for Jonah Game

"IT'S COOL IN THE FURNACE"

Scripture: Daniel 3

King Nebuchadnezzar made a huge golden statue. He ordered everyone in his kingdom to bow down and worship the idol whenever they heard the royal music. The king said that if the people did not worship the idol, they would be thrown into a fiery furnace and would burn to death.

Well, there were three men in the kingdom who refused to bow down to the golden statue: Shadrach, Meshach, and Abednego. These three men served God and said they would not worship anyone but Him. When the king heard this, he became furious. He called for the three to be brought before him.

Shadrach, Meshach, and Abednego still would not worship the golden idol, so King Nebuchadnezzar had them tied up and thrown into the fiery furnace. But God was with them, and they didn't get burned. The king looked into the furnace and saw the men walking around in the furnace. He ordered them to come out. God had protected them so well, they didn't even smell like smoke!

King Nebuchadnezzar realized that the God that Shadrach, Meshach, and Abednego worshipped was the one true God. So the king made a new law that if anyone said anything bad about God, they would be killed. And he promised Shadrach, Meshach, and Abednego that they all three would be promoted in his kingdom.

LEARNING CENTER:

Copy the story. You may want to glue it to ½ of a file folder to make it more durable. Copy, color, and cut out the flames. You will want to record the answers on the back of the flames. (This center is for 1-2 children.)

Directions: Read the story, "It's Cool in the Furnace." Put the flames in the order in which the events took place in the story. The answers are on the back.

Answer Key:

1. King Nebuchadnezzar made a statue.
2. The King ordered everyone to worship the statue.
3. Shadrach, Meshach, and Abednego refused to worship the statue.
4. Shadrach, Meshach, and Abednego told the king they served God.
5. The three men were thrown into the fiery furnace.
6. Shadrach, Meshach, and Abednego walked around in the furnace.
7. The King ordered the three men to come out of the furnace.
8. King Nebuchadnezzar made a new law.
9. Shadrach, Meshach, and Abednego were promoted.

King
Nebuchadnezzar
made a statue.
Shadrach, Meshach,
and Abednego
refused to worship
the statue.
The three men
were thrown into
the fiery furnace.
The king ordered
everyone to worship
the statue.
Shadrach, Meshach,
and Abednego
told the king
they served the
real God.

The king
ordered the three
men to come out
of the furnace.
Shadrach, Meshach,
and Abednego
were promoted.
Shadrach, Meshach,
and Abednego walked
around in the furnace
and didn't get
burned.
King Nebuchadnezzar
made a
new law.

"MOSES OBEYS GOD"

Scripture: Exodus 3, 4

One day Moses was taking care of his father-in-law's sheep. God wanted Moses' attention because God had something very important to tell him. God made a bush catch fire. Moses saw the fire and went over to look at it. When Moses got closer, he saw that the bush was on fire, but it wasn't burning up!

Moses heard God's voice. God said, "Moses, take off your shoes. You are standing on holy ground." Moses was afraid, but God told Moses not to fear Him. Then God told Moses that He felt sad because His children, the Hebrews, were being treated so badly by the Egyptians. He knew that they were suffering.

God told Moses to go to Egypt and get the Hebrews and lead them to a beautiful land. But Moses was afraid that Pharaoh, Egypt's king, would hurt him. Moses was also worried that the Hebrews wouldn't believe that God had really talked to him.

God told Moses to pick up a stick. When Moses picked up the stick, it turned into a snake. Moses threw it down. God told Moses to pick it up by its tail. When he did, the snake turned into a stick again.

God told Moses that the stick and snake would be a sign to the people that Moses really was sent to them by God. So Moses obeyed God and started the long journey to free the Hebrews and lead them to a new land.

LEARNING CENTER:

Copy the story, "Moses Obeys God." Copy, color, and cut out the snakes and sticks. Copy and cut out the word cards. You can record the answers on the back of the cards by writing the corresponding words on them. The sticks and snakes have numbers on the front. This activity can be used by 1-3 players.

Directions: The sentences on the sticks and snakes are missing words. Match the correct word cards with the sentences. The answers are on the back of the cards.

Answer Key:

1. sheep
2. God
3. burning
4. shoes
5. afraid
6. Hebrews
7. Egyptians
8. Egypt
9. Pharaoh
10. stick
11. snake
12. tail
13. stick
14. signs
15. obeyed
16. Egypt/Hebrews

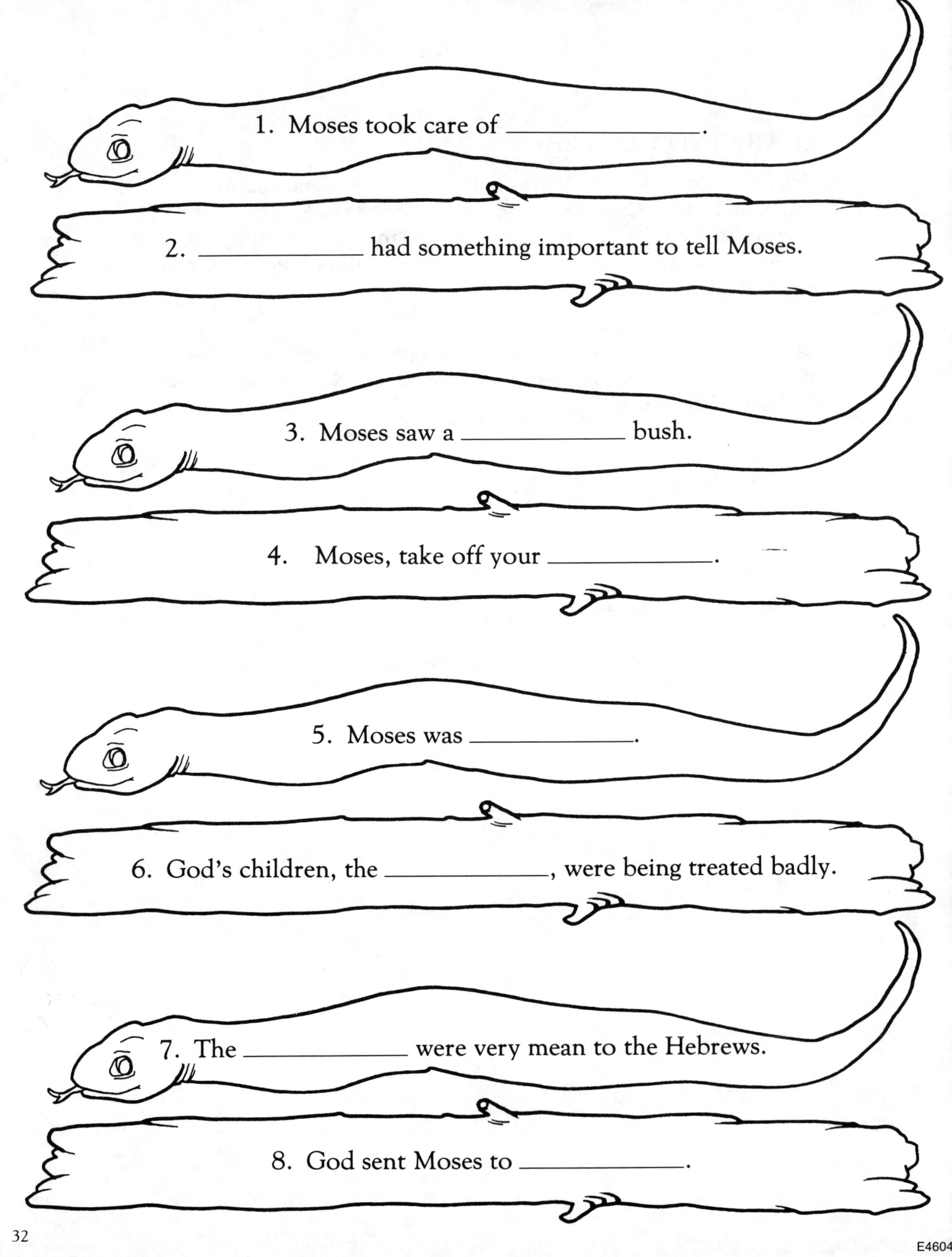
1. Moses took care of ______________.
2. ______________ had something important to tell Moses.
3. Moses saw a ______________ bush.
4. Moses, take off your ______________.
5. Moses was ______________.
6. God's children, the ______________, were being treated badly.
7. The ______________ were very mean to the Hebrews.
8. God sent Moses to ______________.

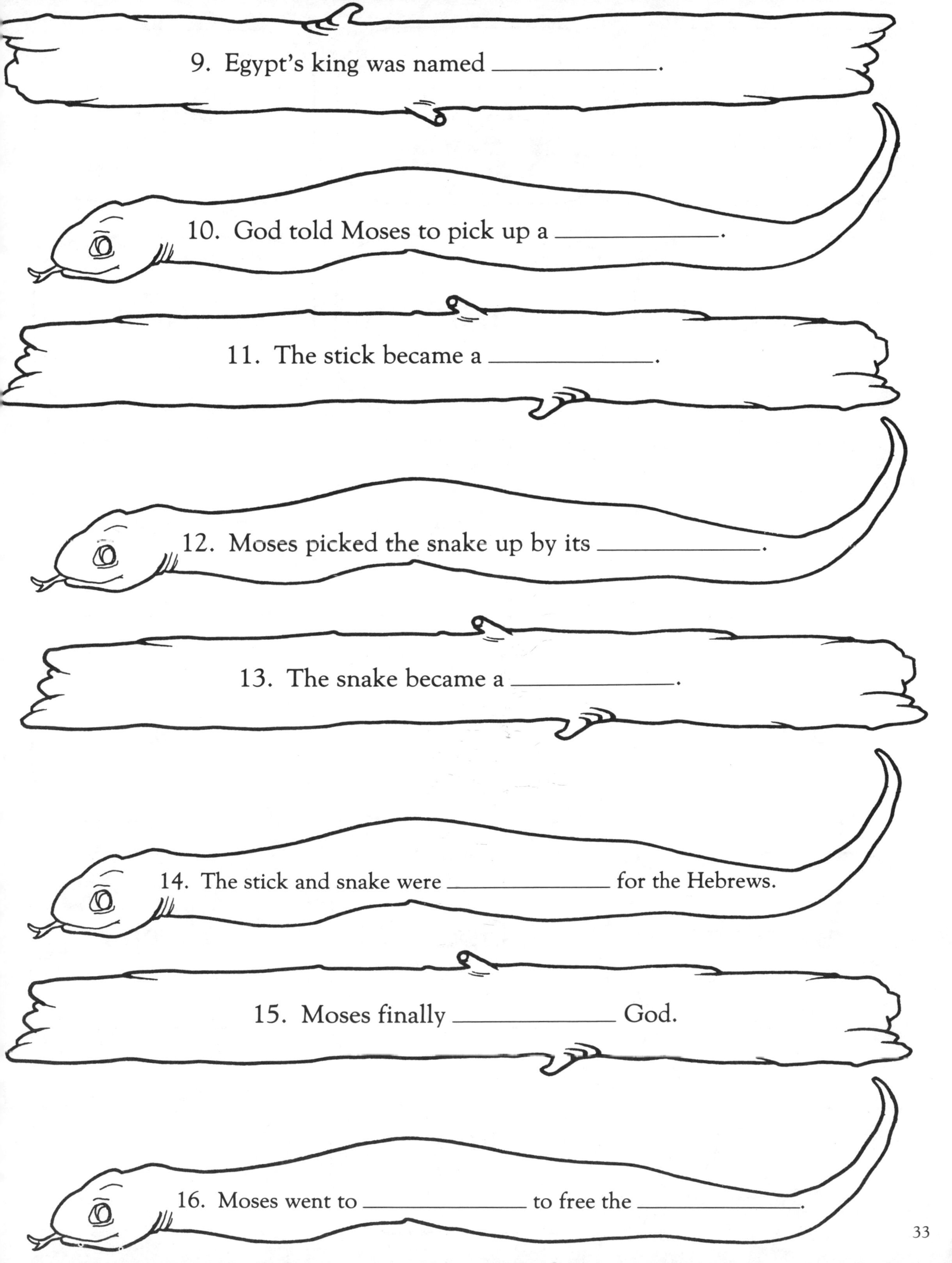
9. Egypt's king was named ____________.
10. God told Moses to pick up a ____________.
11. The stick became a ____________.
12. Moses picked the snake up by its ____________.
13. The snake became a ____________.
14. The stick and snake were ____________ for the Hebrews.
15. Moses finally ____________ God.
16. Moses went to ____________ to free the ____________.

Egypt Hebrews	obeyed	signs
stick	tail	snake
Pharaoh	Egypt	Egyptians
Hebrews	afraid	shoes
burning	God	sheep
	stick	

"JOSEPH HANGS IN THERE"

Scripture: Genesis 37, 41, 44-45

Joseph was a teenager with many older brothers. Jacob, Joseph's father, loved Joseph best of all. Jacob made Joseph a beautiful coat with long sleeves and many colors. This made his brothers jealous, and they began to hate Joseph.

One night, Joseph had a dream. In this dream, Joseph was a ruler, and all of his brothers were bowing down to him. The next day, Joseph told his brothers about the dream. This made his brothers hate him more. But Joseph was kind and stayed true to God.

One day, Jacob sent Joseph to the place where his brothers were taking care of sheep. The brothers saw Joseph from far away and made a plan to kill him. They decided not to kill him, but they did throw him in a deep pit without food or water. They stole his beautiful coat. Later, while they were eating, the brothers saw a group of people going to Egypt. They brought Joseph out of the pit and sold him to these people. Then they killed a goat and dipped Joseph's coat in the blood.

The brothers took the coat to their father. Jacob cried for a long time because he thought a wild animal had killed Joseph.

Joseph had many hard times after being sold to the people going to Egypt. He was even a slave for awhile. But he always obeyed and loved God. One day he became the ruler of Egypt. And in the end his brothers did bow down to him like in his dream.

LEARNING CENTER:

Copy the story, "Joseph Hangs In There." Copy and cut out the boys and coats. You can have the children color them for you. Remind them not to color over the words. Glue the coats to one side of poster board in random order. Glue the boys to the other side in random order. Attach pieces of yarn to the sleeve of each coat (pieces should be long enough to reach opposite side of poster board). Poke a small hole in each boy's hand. The children will put the yarn through the hand of the boy that answers the question on the coat. Do not tie the pieces together. Copy the Answer Key and directions, and glue them to the back of the board.

Directions: Read the story, "Joseph Hangs In There." Read the questions on the coats. Find the boy with the correct answer. Put the yarn from the coat in the hole in that boy's hand. Use the Answer Key to check your answers.

Answer Key:

1. Jacob
2. A beautiful coat
3. They were jealous and hated him.
4. His brothers would bow down to him.
5. Taking care of sheep
6. They planned to kill him.
7. In a deep pit
8. They dipped it in goat's blood.
9. Egypt
10. People going to Egypt
11. He thought an animal had killed Joseph.
12. His brothers
13. He loved and listened to God.